ALL THE PUBLIC RELATIONS YOU NEED TO KNOW

TO RUN A COMPANY SUCCESSFULLY!

All The Public Relations You Need To Know

To Run A Company Successfully!

Dean Sims, APR
Accredited Public Relations
Counselor

Writers Club Press
New York Lincoln Shanghai

All The Public Relations You Need To Know To Run A Company Successfully!

Writers Club Press
an imprint of iUniverse, Inc.

For information address:
iUniverse, Inc.
2021 Pine Lake Road, Suite 100
Lincoln, NE 68512
www.iuniverse.com

ISBN: 0-595-25695-3 (pbk)

ISBN: 0-595-65266-2 (cloth)

Printed in the United States of America

Contents

AUTHOR'S PREFACE

Some of you may get the idea from this book that it dwells too much on the negative, and does not contain enough anecdotes on the remarkable achievements by public relations practitioners.

Let me say this: First, I do not believe all I read or hear about dazzling public relations achievements. PR professionals are especially good at selling ourselves, along with the boss, his company and our clients in general, whom ever pays the bill, gives trust.

Besides, from your point of view, the CEO of a small company, compared with those industry leaders who run General Motors or EXXON, you will go down in history for things you do <u>wrong</u> in handling public relations. Unfortunately, that is the way people are: They tend to remember the failures, seldom the successes.

But…public relations is a vital management tool—if done right; the late Gordon Gilmore, former Iowa news reporter and longtime public relations sparkplug for TWA, said it well to me. I had just apologized for barging in on him in his New York City office, having read where a TWA stewardess had died from a botched abortion by her dentist boyfriend, and a TWA pilot had been charged with raping another airline's stewardess. Gilmore grimaced and said, "Well you can't stop people from being people."

In public relations work, a management service, you don't hit many home runs. Your primary job is to keep the public informed and happy with the organization paying your salary. Your image with, say, the news media, is a tool you need to keep challenged, feeling good, and in business.

Our egos and professional pride are hard to control, but let me remind you of the expression about PR types developing "I shot the bear" complexes.

One thing relative to Americans being world leaders in public relations sophistication: The U.S. is a young country, enterprising at creating new ventures and new ideas, with appropriate rewards for all. No other country has institutions which pay so much to public relations, nor do businesses in other countries pay the money U.S. PR people command. (Only the U.S. allows private ownership of minerals, too.)

I hate the expression, and I have cringed when unknowing executives refer to PR as "that necessary evil."

Only in America is PR considered vital to almost any organization, from airlines to zoos. Non-profits especially need it.

But being Americans, we are also naive in what to expect of public relations. Sometimes people who buy PR services expect miracles, turning their in-house staff people into real basket cases. In turn, the desperate PR people put immature pressures on the media and other groups—like Congress—often leading to corruption and scandal. The waste can be insane.

It is nuts, for example, for a CEO to ask a PR consultant to charge nothing if a strategy does not work out.

"If you don't get that big feature from *The Tribune* that we've been planning on, do we owe you anything for your PR services?"

This is goofy, but every day some CEO asks a question like that one.

Believe it or not, one PR counselor in San Francisco shot and killed his wife, and then himself, over such a situation.

The was the same PR counselor who was fired by a can company for telling the CEO that he could not <u>promise</u> that *The New York Times* would run the photos of three new vice presidents. (Should he have gambled with a lie?)

There is no magic in the public relations profession, mostly hard work and luck, and the ability to communicate effectively. A pleasant personality helps, with winning ways.

It is a damned intangible undertaking—frustratingly so. "Perception" is important; PR makes it possible.

Bosses who want effective public relations should not expect too much—or anything for sure, in the short haul. It takes time and steady building of trust and confidence with the media, your target audience and timing. (Again—even Congress.)

It is wise and good management to have a "crisis management" program in your company, although you will probably never need it. A petroleum refinery had an explosion, and by the time the Chairman heard about it at 7 a.m. from a struggling PR underling who heard it on the midnight radio, the company's image was damaged. Even the wrong employees received national recognition for heroism, and the company got labeled "incompetent" unfairly. It was an act of God but the company was not prepared to properly communicate when the crisis came.

Better safe than sorry, didn't someone say?

The only guarantee you can fairly expect is...BEST EFFORTS. Beyond that, nothing. (If you are dealing with an incompetent PR person, that is a different matter. Either fire him or consult a clinical psychologist.)

One point you must keep in mind as you seek to build a happy image of your company: The bigger you are, the harder you will fall when something goes wrong.

If you look important, you and all of your associates have to be careful because being in the public eye as you are, you can make news accidentally. Good <u>and</u> bad.

Example: A sharp man in Ohio got tired of failing at business, so he organized a company to buy—for pennies on dollars—uncollectable bank loans, then went about a sweet-talk telephone program of wheedling the money out of the debtors. Cash flow seemed great at first since the investment was small, and <u>anything</u> from a beaten-down debtor was better than nothing. The company went ape and publicized everything, including taking thousands of employees on pleasure weekends.

It all sounded sort of screwy, but the media went along. After all, it was feature news—human interest type.

Then on a hot August day, a male employee left work and took his son to the doctor and then left the child in a locked auto in the company parking lot. The boy died from the heat, and it made headlines as law enforcement officials sought to charge the dad with manslaughter. And he was always referred to as an employee of the well-known debt-collection company. It made all the employees look irresponsible and careless. The idea, leaving a child in a locked car on a hot day!

It hurt, and it should have. The good reputation of the company was all puff anyway, now recognized as drawing a bad image of the city…bill-collectors calling all over the country to harass people unable to pay off loans.

It is common sense to "lay low" if you are guilty of doing something sleazy.

As Jefferson said, a role of the newspaper is to "afflict the comfortable."

And reporters, being what they are, rather enjoy alerting the public to things not being as rosy as depicted by a possibly shabby company having a careless employee who let a little kid suffocate.

I suspect, knowing that company's management, that they were tempted to put on a classy funeral for the infant and invite the media out for lunch and hand out news releases.

Publicity gets to be a habit-forming narcotic in such situations.

Consider the successful Kansas City, Missouri, accountant who got a feature story in *The Kansas City Star* on how he jogged all the time. He wanted <u>more</u> publicity, eventually lost his job and became a push-cart junk dealer and a pest around newsrooms, always seeking more print recognition for his running.

Oh, yes—The Ohio debt-collecting company made headlines when it applied for some legislative favors in another state after over $200,000.00 in gifts to surprised legislators.

The news peg was that the company for the past several months had been sending surprise contribution checks to legislators. Now the hook was set.

With a straight face, the retained company lobbyist, a former legislator, said: "Just a coincidence—the contributions and sudden request for legislative aid." (The desired legislation passed!)

THINGS NOT TO BELIEVE ABOUT PUBLIC RELATIONS BUT YOU WILL HEAR THEM ANYWAY!

1. News reporters are not to be trusted.

2. Public relations staff people will say anything to be popular with reporters.

3. Financial publications slant their stories to sell their financial and investment newsletters.

4. Publicity is unpaid advertising and cheaper.

5. If you are a big advertiser, the news media will give you what you want.

6. It is clever to sneak your advertising plugs into the news you make, any way you can.

7. Never trust foreigners, even in their own countries.

8. It is smart to let your attorney also handle your press relations since he knows how to sue people over careless mistakes.

9. Stockholders think only about money; operations bore them.

10. If you shop around, you can buy twice the public relations counsel for half the price.

11. New York financial public relations counselors are in touch with Wall Street every day about your company stock.

12. It is hard to communicate with brokerage firms about making a market for your company's stock.

13. All manufacturers are enemies of the environment.

14. Public speaking is not necessary in corporate communications. Just write it out and hand it out.

15. Don't accept that your company has a problem unless research confirms it; then research the results of what you do to remedy it.

16. You need to know who your media friends and enemies are.

17. Knowledge of accounting is wasted on public relations people who write in annual reports only what they are told.

18. The reporter will be glad to show you his copy before it is printed and eager to send you clippings after the article appears. TV and radio stations will gladly send you gratis recordings.

1

JUST WHAT IS (ARE) PUBLIC RELATIONS

First, it is damnably intangible!

It is hard to nail down, although some sophisticated, overeducated counselors seek to overcomplicate it with such things as opinion research and predictions of human behavior. Many CEOs buy such programs only because they feel that if they do not understand or follow the PR counselors, it must be the CEOs own stupidity.

I have grown so weary of some of my contemporaries, all introverts, launching into pipe-puffing tirades on obtaining public relations goals for clients by long-range strategies that are both impossible and expensive.

The busy, fickle and impatient public wants informative answers NOW!

Tomorrow, the public will itch to know something else, so be alert and stay on top (or make sure somebody on your Communications staff is on top).

There are lots of ways to communicate with designated publics…stockholders, employees and customer prospects, and lots more. Families of employees, for example.

You do the following in this order:

A. Determine the problem.

B. Prepare the message or activity.

C. Choose the medium, and set the budget.

D. GO!

E. Evaluate the playback, results of surveys.

F. Keep something going so your message is remembered and updated.

We were hired by a large national firm to create good will for them with selected U.S. Senators. We started by learning all about the senators, their colleges, families, hometowns—and favorite charities. We began making donations in the name of the client to the charities, wishing the groups well. We never did ask for anything of the senators, nor took credit for the donations. But we and a client staffer always showed up to smile and say hello.

It was a good PR program and not too expensive. The relationship blew up when the client got anxious and demanded we move in for our rewards from the senators. We got fired, but not before I attended a New York City reception where one nationally known member of Congress got up and publicly thanked the company for $350,000 it raised to pay his debts, and then he pledged never to vote against the best interests of the company.

HORRORS! I still cannot believe it.

COMMUNICATION is the very heart of public relations, just as it is the very heart of civilization. PR people should be professional communicators, good writers, good speakers, good thinkers and planners, and very creative for developing unique approaches for talking to and hearing from the chosen audience the client has in mind.

We use music and jingles, and advertising, and videotapes, audio tapes, pamphlets, movies, brochures and booklets. Even the logo trademark must have public appeal. Even the corporate name.

We received a call one time from a troubled company's board member. "How much will you charge to change the name of our company?" he asked. "No", he corrected himself. "Management would never let us do that. How much would you charge just to lighten the spots on our company's bad reputation?"

Books had been written about the company's management bilking wealthy Americans out of millions of dollars. They had a long list of federal convictions, including mail fraud, but had used a clever attorney to stay out of jail except briefly.

Public relations should be an ongoing program, not putting out fires every now and then.

Americans are well-informed, fair-minded people who support winners who do right, sell and service good products and stand for high principles.

You can't beat being for the flag, motherhood and apple pie, and telling the truth and not shortchanging your friends and associates. That can be expected of us all.

Nobody admires a drunk or womanizer, or even a woman who seduces men for business reasons.

And if you expect the public to support you, you must support the public. Go find things needing your input and then do it smilingly and graciously. (Many companies have people who do this and nothing else. Smile, that is, and shake hands.)

Treat media people respectfully since they have the communications tools you need to get your good story told. Find writers who can write your news releases as well or better than the media people can write news. Be thoughtful, considerate and polite but try to talk <u>news</u>, if you possibly can. Media people appreciate getting tips on stories other than your own. Give a little inside gossip about your industry and what you see the future holding for the media audiences.

Whether you practice the fundamentals of public relations yourself or not, you <u>must</u> understand what public relations is and does, to manage your company properly.

Abe Lincoln is credited with pointing out that nothing good will occur without public support. Thomas Jefferson said he would rather live in a country with no government than a country with no newspaper.

An early railroader said, "The public be damned!" We know how he felt, but he was wrong because the informed American public is one of our greatest national resources.

In all my years in public relations, I have never looked upon any segment of the public as a body to be exploited. Informed, yes, and looked to for support, but never to be exploited. Those who do will be hurt in many ways.

When you think of public relations, it is natural to think first of "publicity." And publicity is dangerous, not to be entered into lightly or even heavily. One client once said to me, "You should have told me I was grabbing a bear by the tail to get involved in generating so much publicity."

If you don't feel you understand public relations, let somebody else be responsible for it. Nothing makes news people more nervous than an up-tight CEO. They will think you are hiding something, which you are: a shallow understanding of how publicity works. There is an art to correcting a stated mistake without embarrassment or showing a lack of control over your company's actions.

Frankly, it is nearly impossible to understand what news is unless you have worked for a news medium, actually getting the news, element by element, and passing it on to the public so they understand it.

You're more or less a dead duck if you use your spokesman capacity for something really self-serving, misleading or dishonest.

I erred one time by announcing my own firm would hold a series of European investment conferences, by bringing a few dozen foreign investors to town to hear presentations from local companies that would sign up to pay fees to meet the investors on their own turf. Only a few signed up locally, which meant we would not have sufficient funds to bring the investors over. A local newspaper business editor suspected what I was up to and called weekly to let me know he was waiting for the conference date and names of those on the program. I had to admit to him I had failed in my concept. Because I was forthright about it, he did not print that the meetings had been called off. Perhaps he should have.

Never underestimate the perceptions of reporters. That is their job. And my job is to know what a client or reporter means and NOT exactly what they say.

It is a dangerous business not to be messed with without experience or, at least, knowledge of others' experiences. That, by the way, is the purpose of this book.

2

JUST DO IT YOURSELF?

So you think you can do it all yourself?

You don't need a public relations staff or even outside counselors?

By golly, you know and like people, and you were terrific at communicating when you were in high school and college.

Why should you let somebody else's personality and socializing substitute for yours? After all, you're the boss, and nobody better forget it.

Well, maybe you're right. But probably not.

Let me put it this way: Your time is much too valuable to devote much of it to routine communicating, regardless of its importance. If your company should stumble, you would be remembered as the egomaniac who was always in the headlines, who spent so much time commenting that he let the company go to pot. (The media are fickle in appreciating even their friends.)

We have all heard the saying, "The lawyer who represents himself in court has a fool for a client."

One of the most successful board chairmen of a NYSE-listed company absorbs all the outside counsel he can soak up and then does what he thinks is best for the company. He is such an outgoing personality and informal communicator that he would really rather not have a PR firm's name on his news releases, but he knows the third-party arrangement is better for his company, and ultimately himself.

Even media people can be unfair when an important person is too visible to them. They're often too quick to brand a person an "egomaniac" when he is trying to cooperate.

Now, please pay attention to this often-taken misstep by CEOs who feel sort of smartypants about thinking of public relations, then doing it. They hire news people on a freelance basis to do their publicity work, starting with their own medium.

This will lead to disaster not only for them when their bosses learn of it (and they will) but for you also for <u>corrupting</u> members of the Fourth Estate.

Even the news people will hold you in contempt for degrading them along with yourself. The contempt from them will get you lots of bad press, and you have no defense. You know you took the low road, the simple method of getting what you want, admittedly, for good and proper business reasons.

In talks on public relations and news groups, I always praise news people as being the most honest of any profession—at least <u>trying</u> to be fair, honest and objective. I mean it!

Never even consider buying a news person to do your publicity. It is awful to contemplate what a bad idea it is.

A Midwestern newspaper business editor tempted a car dealer to sell him a new one at wholesale or less, then unveiled a case of champagne for himself at holiday time. Then, his disgust with himself suddenly boiled over, and he never wrote a nice thing about the car dealer again.

The car dealer has never figured out what happened.

It was just a bad idea between two people, both wanting something from the other and it could have been expected to go sour. And the sooner the better.

3

THE PUBLIC RELATIONS STAFF

One head of a public company I know went nearly thirty years with no in-house public relations staff, but he grew impatient at outside counselors approaching him with sales pitches every now and then. The counselors made him insecure with all their aggressive ideas and outside media contacts. How could he be sure they were being loyal for all the trust and money he gave them?

Admittedly, this chairman had good but unique ideas, and they worked. He made up his mind he wanted a wild animals on his annual report covers. He did it and got lots of favorable response for the points he made with the unusual artwork, helping him tell the story he wanted to stockholders. It fit his sportsman personality. The outside counselors went ape because none of them took the time to understand their role with such a chief executive.

So he hired himself a steady inside communicator, one with no original ideas and no ambition beyond normal retirement with a pension. He did what the boss wanted, right, wrong or maybe. It was a happy match.

A major problem with building your own staff is that you often can hire people with either too little or too much experience. The former often have ambitions of their own and use the job and trust and budget to further their own identities. After leaving Associated Press, my first

PR job, for a utility company, had me issuing a news release, which I did. But I didn't know my boss wanted to approve my copy before I put it out. My release was canceled with the 350 newspapers, then was formally approved with no changes and then sent out again. I learned something.

My inexperienced thinking was naive: "But I am fresh from the AP, and you hired me for my news writing ability."

The overly experienced types do not have the patience to let executives tell them how to do the jobs they were hired to do with their contacts of many years standing. They do not want to learn anything new, and if the boss had the experience, he could do it himself or hire some kids just out of school to train in his own image.

And like news people, older PR practitioners often develop bad habits like drinking, womanizing, lying to save a hassle, and even living off expense accounts.

An eighth-grade dropout executive made a good point with me once: "Try to remember who is paying your salary when you need to decide whether the newspaper or the company is most right."

A wise, older general counsel of a company where I was a young but energetic staff member for public relations took me to task for making a silly mistake. It took me three minutes to explain to him the circumstances that made the mistake the fault of somebody else. He leaned back in his fine chair and sighed, "I am so happy to know you, one who unlike the rest of us, never makes mistakes. You are a remarkable fellow. I am sleepless sometimes over the mistakes I make. You will go far."

I blushed and still do over that incident where a fine executive taught me a lesson I needed to know.

Showing the common sense of maturity, most executives today allow PR people be the spokesperson for the company. This avoids the hassles and pitfalls of multiple sources trying to convey a single message for the company, especially to the news media.

If you hire PR staff members, give them money and dignity and support their continuing education through organizations like the Public Relations Society of America and the International Association of Business Communicators. Send them to management conferences and let them attend yours.

Another great compliment I had in growing up on the corporate job was when a board of directors met secretly to make a great newsworthy decision and I was not invited so took a few hours of holiday on a nearby beach. One of the directors, a former public relations staffer and ex-newsman, said to the chairman, "If you don't trust the bastard enough to let him attend your meetings, get rid of him!"

I shall always cherish that compliment by Emmet F. Butler of the Maytag Company. It made my job better—and me better, too.

This is a good time to discuss backgrounds of the people you hire for staff. Most journalism schools offer majors in public relations or business communications.

Women are more productive than men, are less competitive with the policy-level. Men are more temperamental, women easy to get on with. Women put personal lives aside whereas men put their families ahead of the job nearly always.

I like PR people with news backgrounds for four reasons:

1. Former news people are resourceful and persistent. They never give up on finding an answer.

2. They are skilled communicators, crowding a lot of information into a few well-chosen words.

3. They are perceptive. They know how to get information, not from what you say but from what you meant.

4. They will keep you out of trouble because of their journalistic training in pursuing truth and objectivity.

A utility CEO I knew in Michigan made up his mind to have a newsman on his staff. He went to the very top, finding a Pulitzer Prize winner. The new hire made a good PR staffer but did not work very hard. He did not have to. He just went around with the boss and took bows in the newsrooms. Fortunately, he also did some good writing.

4

OUTSIDE PUBLIC RELATIONS COUNSEL

Retaining the services of an acknowledged professional is how you get the public relations experience you do not have the time or resources to hire and train.

The chairman of the biggest client we ever had, 500 miles from my office, said, "Staff people get underfoot with their crazy ideas they have to keep their jobs intact. All I need to know is that you can do my jobs best, let me have your telephone number, and then I can get from you only what I need at the price I can pay."

Unless your ego is tough and your office walls soundproof, you may not like being in the presence of "powerful" public relations counselors, probably from New York, LA or Chicago.

The former chairman of Carl Byoir & Associates said bosses are afraid to death of counselors who cannot help their "I shot the bear!" complexes. No matter what they do for the CEO clients, they take credit for it.

This is the result of immaturity, inexperience, insecurity—or often a dumb client in the hands of a skillful counselor.

If you are a client, get treated with respect and get help to actually do and say the things your PR counselor wants. (If it fits you, of course.)

Once our firm was fired by an executive who felt I "talked down" to him on public relations matters. Another time the boss who fired us said, "I don't feel comfortable around such people."

Neither of them was the ideal client, either. Both had deep problems of insecurity.

Public relations counseling is a team effort with a client whose chemistry harmonizes with yours. He or she does the job as the boss, and your job is to assist discretely in the ways needed, which will vary all over the map.

As a consultant, twice in my life have I had CEO clients, a woman and a man, who hated me. The woman got her job as head of a utility company by sleeping with other directors when she survived her late boss in actually running the company. The other had lied horribly about his background in order to get the top job, and I knew from putting together his biography that much he claimed was untrue. Without my involvement, both ultimately were exposed and terminated.

Another company chairman took me gently to task when he had to fire a director and subsidiary president over unsavory behavior, mainly extramarital. I had known about it because the errant executive had confided in me that a secretary he had dallied with was blackmailing him.

I did not know I was being paid to be a spy and hatchet man, and I had other company officers I wanted to trust me. This is a point still debated. How far do I go in earning and keeping the trust of the head man?

Most important in hiring a consultant is finding somebody you like and respect, who gives you his best, and works intimately with you. You do not always have to take his advice. Flatter him occasionally and pay him well. Share jokes and friends. Keep him casually informed even about trivia. Do not be too quick to criticize. Remember that his

PR contacts are <u>his</u> and it is important to you that they be solid and in working order. Remember also that the news media and other opinion leaders must respect your consultant for the consultant to be effective for you.

Whether the consultant has a news background or not, he or she needs to have easy access to newspaper, radio and TV news rooms and the confidence, perhaps even admiration, of the news people. Only a consultant with at least a knack for or appreciation of news media life can do the job.

Frequently, I remind myself to throttle back and shut up in dealing with clients. You might miss something important if you do not listen to all the client wants to say, and most are polite enough not to remind you of this.

Where does counselor enthusiasm and common sense leave off?

I know. I know.

With time and successful production, all clients will learn to like and trust the counselor fully.

Pay good money for counselor services; keep them economically secure. Make it impossible for them to trade you in for a better-paying client.

A chairman once turned me down for a monthly retainer three times what he had in mind. He said, "We may keep you poor, but we will keep you honest."

Yeah? This is the only publicly held client company whom we got printers on their work to pay us <u>35</u> percent commissions instead of the standard 15 percent. We earned it!

And another savvy comment you should remember in hiring a consultant: "Remember always that those outsiders instrumental in making you look good can just as easily make you look bad, with exactly the same tools."

The head of an investment company called me in a panic that a public relations firm had just fired him because as chairman he had tried to help make the media happy. We took on his firm, and the firm grew and prospered while ours withered on a small retainer that needed to be increased. So I asked for more money.

"Consider our relationship terminated at this moment," said the banker-type, "and, therefore, you will lose less money."

The last I heard he was making and keeping lots of money, without an outside PR firm helping him. He could not "let go."

After half a century in public relations, I no longer blame clients but myself for not being quick enough to avoid problems of communications in getting well paid for our services.

Oh, yes, the above client stayed out of town six weeks after a securities commission accused him of misstatements in a filing with them. He was not dishonest, he just allowed a low-paid staffer to prepare the return instead of taking it to an attorney who specializes in such matters.

Because public relations counselors need to be aggressive and articulate, clients hiring one often find themselves between two or more counseling firms fighting for the account.

Ethics be damned when it comes to business with large fees and little production demanded, often loosely managed by an unsophisticated and dreamy client.

Inside the counseling firms, there are usually cut-throat fights between personnel over trivia—like money or recognition or power over others and money.

We were hired at the very outset of its work by a large Colorado-based company to do national publicity directed toward potential users of the company's services. The CEO did not know many people in public relations, so we were lucky and really spread our wings. We stationed staff in four different cities, and in St. Louis, Mo., we hired a branch of a large PR firm based in New York City. While the St. Louis branch was on our payroll, the head of the New York headquarters went calling on our client's second-level management. We would up terminated, but only for six months, during which the New York firm did little but bluster, put down, ridicule and arrange a Buffalo, N. Y., radio interview. Buffalo? There was no connection.

While we waited in the wings for our client to come back, I called the chairman of the New York PR firm and told him what his president had done. "I don't know what the hell is going on around here anymore," he lamented.

Another time, we hired a woman heading a Washington, D.C. PR firm to do some Washington work for a group of our clients wanting to meet with Congressmen and the Washington press. She addressed our clients at a breakfast meeting: "You folks can do a lot better in public relations by coming to me direct and avoid the problems you have with your present public relations counsel with no knowledge of Washington, and I can give you full-time for half what you are paying now."

I didn't believe it! Neither did our clients who suggested we choose our professional friends better in the future.

Another time we had a large client try to go from private to public ownership, and the client chairman felt we could use some New York PR help, so a New York firm was hired to "help" us. It was a bitter experience, with total lack of cooperation between our two firms.

The client executive vice president called me: "I have never seen such professional disrespect in my life!"

We were criticized for everything by the New York firm's principals, even lousing up a new logo and some proposed advertising, as well as everything else.

What the New York firm did not understand was that we were in the city of the client, 2,000 miles away, and we spoke the same language as the client.

When our client decided not to go public, the CEO told the New York firm it was no longer needed. But, wait a minute. There is a $120,000 per annum basic fee contract, and $60,000 is due as a second installment. Read the contract. You can cancel, but you pay anyway.

The client CEO who did the deal based on advice from a Houston friend turned the problem over to the chief financial officer, who called me: "Those guys are so lousy, that they make you look good."

(The client did not pay, invited litigation, but outside NYC the ethic is "no work, no pay.")

A Chicago PR firm called on the telephone that we had been selected to represent it with the Dallas office of one of its clients. We went over to Dallas and the client CEO for the region said, "Go to hell!"

I called the Chicago PR official and was told he could not pay us anyway, that the whole thing was a trial balloon to see what we might work out for ourselves. "You obviously are not good at selling," said the PR official with ridicule.

In summary, be prepared for slick overpromising when you go East, particularly for PR counsel.

I took a New York PR firm staffer with me to Alaska once (at our client management's urging), and I returned home after a week, job done. The New Yorker shacked up for another week with a friend, and when he wasn't bedded, he wrote critical letters to my boss about how naive I was and absolutely lost.

But I did the job and was praised by my client's general counsel, who judged me by the results.

You have to watch out, and as one client said to me once, "You need to know you are grabbing a bear by the tail when you hire any kind of public relations counsel."

PR counselors can be a disgrace to the business, ethically, and the larger the firm, the more CEO heads you find rolling—and clients being lost and stolen.

5
UNDERSTANDING THE NEWS MEDIA

You probably feel that news reporters are a grimy lot of underpaid, hard-drinking, swaggering intellectual bullies.

Well, some are; some aren't.

True, most do not use their powers of public influence the way YOU would. (Thank goodness!)

But today, the young'ns with broadcast and PR degrees, made to work for news media by economic necessity, do not want to work very hard, as if news is something that is thought not to spoil if it is done next week instead of last night.

I once wrote a story for the Burlington, Iowa, *Hawk-Eye Gazette*, and a male reader got so angry that he went home and shot his shotgun at his wife and her visiting lover. He peppered her seat as she bent over to get into the racing boyfriend's auto and blew a hole in the side of his car with the second shot. The jury acquitted the angry husband—who had a right to be, they said—and so he went after his ex-wife (by then) with a knife. Later, he tried rat poison. I do not know where it ended.

My act was irresponsible. It was a slow news day, and I tried too hard to help the managing editor to fill the space around the ads.

Reporters are more responsible today, but they still are menaces when they naively write about business and do the obits. I am often shocked at how deceased bums I know actually held British knighthoods or were fighter aces of World War II, though born about the time of Pearl Harbor in 1941.

A reporter for one of the world's great newspapers wrote of a CEO who said that his company would make no profit for at least five years. The chairman was trying to make a "what if" point with the reporter. Directors and stockholders screamed.

The late J. R. D. Tata of India was interviewed by a great New York newspaper, and they labeled him "Lord Tata," who was his uncle. The chairman of Air India etc., thought it funny.

An Oklahoma newspaper sent a reporter out to interview a man, and the feature appeared, drawing informed calls that the subject had died five years earlier.

Radio reporters are okay since they are older and unfit for TV cameras. They ask good questions and listen to your answers, even by telephone.

TV news people are "talking heads" or entertainers who do not know news and do not have air time to do it well, anyway. (No wonder the public gets most information from TV. They do not have to think, just hear and believe.)

News people do have lofty objectives of objectivity and truth, which they have drummed into them all the time. Maybe they do not all understand it, but they say they do.

I wrote a daily column for a newspaper and felt, at 23, I had to use it for small-time crusades and investigative disclosures. My problems were I did not know all the background needed, and my publisher was a social climber who wanted no enemies. (Actually, I think I was a misguided enemy of free enterprise because the system had not yet done much for me.)

Patience, Dean, patience. Remember your father did well in the mining business as an eighth grade dropout, and he sent you to college, with all the fraternity trimmings. (But still no car!)

You have to like news and news people in order to get along with them, give in to their terms, support their Press Club activities—but don't offer them gifts of money. The latter gesture will destroy you. (I see socialites doing it with society editors and writers, but it is still wrong.)

Learn to be available for comment or explanation when a reporter asks you, but be prepared also for your friends to ridicule you for being a "headline snatcher." They are just jealous, and you can be proud you were available to a reporter who had an assignment from an editor to complete.

The late John W. Colt of *The Kansas City Star* was always being sent out to the Union Station when Will Rogers was coming through. Rogers would never say anything funny, saving it all for his next vaudeville appearance. Finally, Colt told him he would lose his job if he got no story. Rogers pointed to the new and towering K. C. War Memorial: "Hey, quite a silo you've got there." At last, a quote.

Find out when your newspaper editorial board meets and sit in to talk about your views on some current event you know something about. You have to wrangle an invitation, but you will learn what makes their editorial policy and why they have views that you probably do not understand or may not agree with.

The Toledo Blade editorial staff had a lot of laughs over readers who disagreed with their editorials. Instead of writing letters, the readers would cancel their subscriptions. Soon they re-subscribed since they did not feel comfortable in life without a daily newspaper.

When Bernard Judy was editor of *The Toledo Blade*, a disagreeable reader executive asked him what the newspaper policy was to be so against certain issues.

"Frankly, we don't understand the issues as you do,"

Judy said, "but simply feel that if you are so against what we say, you must be guilty of something that is not right."

Above all, as a CEO, you must be interested in and informed about the news. Otherwise, you come off as a dummy who must not be a very capable executive.

You could do worse than put your news favorites, or unfavorites, on the mailing list to get your company employee and stockholder publications.

I know a corporate vice president in Kansas City who got fired over fighting with his company's public relations people over what to name the house organ. He also refused to let the city newspaper know what company employees were doing at Christmas to help needy families, after the newspaper pleaded for help with Christmas edition stories to twang the heartstrings of readers.

If you don't really understand news or like news people, act as if you do, or let somebody else do it for you—but eventually the faults will catch up with you. Remember, the media have the last word, even those damned obituaries that are the final and lasting memorial your family and friends have about you.

My conscience still bothers me occasionally over the ethics we practiced in dealing with a high-roller CEO in his periodic interviews by *The Wall Street Journal,* known for its informed and hardworking reporters and accurate printing of news. This CEO's company had stock listed and traded on the New York Stock Exchange and was in the business where highs and lows in stock prices were routine. The CEO spokesman could not help putting some "promo" into most things he said to the *WSJ* because he felt he had the right to tell report-ers what he wanted as long as it was "generally true."

After every interview, the reporter would go back to his home base, and I would call him to clarify the information he had been given. On occasion what the boss had said wasn't exactly true or false. The spokesman knew he had some hostile stockholders in, say, New Jersey waiting to get some good news on their investments.

Finally, the chairman retired, and the executive vice president became chairman, and the *WSJ* reporters told him how much they appreciated the past clarifications and hoped he would profit from it. Annually, the new chairman and I would go for Dutch-treat dinners with the group of *WSJ* reporters in their home city of Dallas. Soon, they were calling him for comment on news he had nothing directly to do with. He earned their trust.

I am not especially proud of what I did, but somebody needed to do something to clean up the chairman's quotes. I still feel that investors deserve the truth about the companies they would invest in. Company spokesmen should tell the truth, no matter how much it hurts. It is ille-gal not to.

Which reminds me, I have never known the SEC to be wrong in censoring publicly held companies for their rules violations.

And before we leave the news media, please DO NOT EVER ask the reporter to show you his copy before he turns it in to his Editor. That violates ethics, meaning they are free to misquote you or say a few things wrong, all in protection of their independence and objectivity. And it is EVEN WORSE to ask the reporter to see that you are sent clippings on what finally appears in print, or even tapes from broad-casts. I have seen reporters so perplexed over these two innocent requests that they threw their notes away and reported nothing.

If you expect reporters to respect you, you must first show respect for them and the vital work they do.

It is too much to expect news people to understand the trusting, respectful, dedicated relationship between company management and their inside or outside PR people.

Because a veteran and brilliant news journalist knew a client's field better than I, I offered the newsman a nifty fee to do a freelance profile of the CEO for <u>another</u> publication. First, the newsman said he wanted a gift of a new computer he had needed for some time.

I paid the newsman, did not buy him the computer, and the other publication ran the client's profile. The client never paid us our $3,500 fee because his wife convinced him that he could have gotten the same publicity on his own, being a socialite and philanthropist.

I am still speechless, just glad I did not buy the computer.

A talented woman in another city is a gifted and established magazine feature writer whom we retain from time to time. She also works as a reporter for small newspapers who pay her very little for her time, so she is busy going in circles. I pay her well enough to demand the best of her time for our clients.

The problem I have is that I cannot seem to reach her in understanding that when she takes our clients' money, she needs to follow through on the articles she writes and submits. Good articles have a habit of just disappearing after a submission or two. I expect her to keep trying, and we will keep paying her until she hits a publisher with the desired results. We feel responsible—and should.

The problem is mine, buying a quality service for reasonable rates but without the sophistication of making sure corporate clients get what they pay for. I would rather use this writer, follow up with her, keep her motivated than I would somebody who overpromises or overcharges. Either one's bloopers could cost me credibility, so I will assume responsibility for the former.

One time a *Reader's Digest* Editor found that a freelance writer for them was charging me his travel expenses in addition to what they were paying him. The article and writer both went down the drain, and we all looked bad to the client who really had a good story to tell.

Even when you know the communications business, it is hard to get along with freelance writers, keeping them producing for the story you hope they see and the money they get.

I will close this news media chapter with one of the most perfect anecdotes involving corporate press relations I have ever heard. A big company in Ohio planned the dedication of a new office building and did not invite *The Toledo Blade* to attend the ceremony because company management disliked the *Blade's* editorial policy. The State Editor of the *Blade* called the PR manager of the company and commented that he was aware of the missing invitation but their correspondent would cover it for them and another newspaper that had been invited. "We have your press kit on the new building, and it does not say how much it cost. How much?"

"We don't know!" retorted the PR manager, a Wyoming house organ editor new in town.

So the *Blade* carried the story: "A company spokesman said they did not know how much the new building cost.

Served them right, and, once again, the press always has the last word.

Sure, the novice PR manager was demoted, but his act was not just his fault. It was company policy not to like *The Toledo Blade*.

A final note: The policy changed when the big company chairman was put in touch with the *Blade's* publisher and they got along famously, joined together for a new medical school in Toledo, among other good things.

It is corporate image suicide to have a corporate policy that challenges a news medium to fight back.

6

PUBLIC RELATIONS IN MARKETING

Even though your company is selling a quality product or service, it is good to have a top-management policy of being extra nice and communicative with your customers. Keep them feeling good!

Although as a youth I did not like the suffocating taste of Ovaltine, I liked the Little Orphan Annie prizes I got for mailing in labels. I had no car so did not buy gasoline, but I thrilled at being a member of the Jimmy Allen flying aces of Skelly Oil Company. Remember that other product's secret-decoder badges?

Airlines will cooperate with you when you take customers and prospects on trips to see your products at work, eating steaks and drinking scotch along the way.

Speaking of airlines, I have seen some of their customer relations policies backfire on them, mainly inviting transportation managers on gala free flights. The managers worked hard to shut out all others in their companies from such trips, so the top brass would simply cut down the tripping-around privileges of the managers. Greedy possessive people ruining a good program. TWA had a lot of trouble over this since at one time theirs were the finest overseas junkets, matched only by the now defunct Braniff, Eastern and Pan American. (Does that tell you something?)

But it is still important to involve public relations in marketing programs.

Just add some restraint, which is something marketing and ad people are a little short of. Being closer to top management, PR people do it better.

The institutional advertising you do is the face behind the products and services you sell. It pays to brag a little in such ads about your history, management and policies. If you are patriotic, that helps. Tell the story as you see it, being the CEO.

And the greatest element in marketing public relations is usually "new product" publicity in appropriate journals. This is some of the best "free" advertising you can get, although there is nothing really free about publicity. You need the services of a good product news writer and photographer.

Having an aggressive, talented products publicity person available pays great dividends.

The same goes to a lesser degree for the services you sell.

It is routine, of course, no matter what you sell, to have brochures and pamphlets. You can, however, waste a lot of money on audiovisuals nobody will take the time to view or listen to.

If you do invest in audiovisuals, maybe you can snag some time on a TV channel somewhere, if you put human interest in the story. TV burns up a lot of footage in its many cable channels going around the clock.

One company I know tripled its manufacturing plant size after an article on its new product appeared in *Reader's Digest*.

Really, all the world seems waiting for a new product or service, so you use good public relations help to let the world know what you've got, what it will do for them.

And, please, exercise good taste and professionalism when you communicate…and don't puff up the facts. You may be asked to certify test results.

7

CORPORATE GOOD CITIZENSHIP

No matter haw smug you are about running your own show without attention to your community and industry neighbors, you are crippled if you aren't well thought of by those two publics.

If your hometown doesn't know and like you, this negative message will be heard around the world. It will precede you in all you do.

If you aren't an industry affairs player, this hurts you, too.

Louis Ruthenberg, founder and late chairman of Servel, Inc., once observed that company managements must take active roles, in non-profit industry organizations because indirectly through their educational work, members of the industry can make profits.

Time and again, the first folks the public call to find information regarding a company they had never heard of is the chamber of commerce, and an enthusiastic report from there starts that ball rolling in your favor.

A company chairman I know was poorly thought of in his home city because he kept a low profile and just did his work without any community involvement. Suddenly, the SEC dropped a charge on him, and the local media did not know him, so they ran reports of the charges without compassion. The chairman did not know what to do about it, so he hid from scrutiny. When he went to jail, even the judge lamented that he seemed nicer than the charges against him indicated.

Now the chairman hates everybody, sneaks around town, face cast down, shoulders stooped.

If he had been acknowledged as a community leader and a supporter of worthy causes, his damnation would have been less severe.

As a matter of fact, being involved in community affairs with your peers helps keep you straight, like a Boy Scout living by the Scout Oath and the Scout Laws.

It is a wonderful idea to develop your own employees' leadership reservoir by letting them get leadership training in community service groups. Such training costs you very little and pays rewards in all kinds of ways.

I know a city that had an impotent chamber of commerce because the staff head was always a formerly unemployed company executive everybody knew but who knew nothing about chamber work. When the last such misfit retired, a professional and aggressive chamber manager was brought in. He told the board that hired him: "If you hire me, it will mark the end of ribbon clerks serving in leadership positions. We want the best, very top in management to be involved, or I will soon show you my coattails. I am ambitious, and you better be, too."

Everybody did what the new manager wanted, and he was still doing great running a great chamber and after 34 years. He had personally helped many companies find themselves for the better in the community and helped them expand their markets.

A true introvert inherited his grandfather's furniture manufacturing plant, and he unexpectedly was chosen a delegate to a White House conference for three days. It changed his life, and the last I heard, he was visiting in Birmingham, England, for European outlets for his Midwest-made furniture. He is a growing tiger of leadership, even has employee meetings and presides at local service clubs in charge of programs. Community involvement changed him and made the community better with stronger employment, increased tax payments and a finer industrial complex.

When you choose local charities to support with company money and manpower, find your own. If you merely join with many other companies, you will not stand out, wasted resources.

We were involved in finding a community home for a charity hospital in California, and we involved the chairman-founder of a company in being its patron. It went great until two other similar religious charities ran the hospital out of town and left our chairman-founder high and dry. Being a good citizen, he turned his efforts and financial influence to building a brand new Red Cross headquarters building for his state.

Community groups, like all non-profit, do-good activities, bring out the best and worst in people involved in leadership. You see the glorious and the petty at work, and you have to ignore the negative and get on with the positive.

And when you choose your company people to be in community leadership roles, think twice about naming either bankers or lawyers. Both professions have the freedoms to hurt people more than help them. There is little broad public trust for either, and the 21st century will find it even worse.

Amen. Amen, and turn the page now before I get petty about accountants and their narrow little minds.

Oh, yes, public relations people, like news people, make lousy community leaders since they do not have the patience the job requires. It is all "rat now!" and clanging of bells and blaring of trumpets.

And beware of leaning on political types who may talk issues to death and actually accomplish little.

8

STOCKHOLDER PUBLIC RELATIONS

There are two ways CEOs can look at stockholders: people you love and nurture and respect, or people you consider a necessary evil and stay away from.

I hate to tell you that the Securities and Exchange Commission (SEC) does not support you in the latter attitude.

Once we had a chairman accuse us of catering to his New York Stock Exchange stockholders "in order to earn bigger commissions, and time and art charges, and printing, from the prettier mailings going to stockholders."

Obviously, you need to build stockholder trust in how you are using their money, and you certainly must work hard to give them a fair return on their earnest investment.

I recently was called back to town to address the annual meeting of stockholders of an OTC (over the counter) stock company, mostly small, ma and pa type investors. They were taking the hide off the chairman when I walked in, the company being in the red two years longer than he had promised them. Watch selling stock to small investors, and watch those promises you make! Such intimacy does breed contempt!

In my talk, I told the audience I heard what they said, and I thought they were being prematurely unfair with a good young company that would in time justify their faith. What else could I do?

The founder of MAPCO Inc., remembered until his retirement those original stockholders who gave him their money, and he was devoted to them. When he retired and we had helped him stay in touch with the stockholders, he was succeeded by a chairman who put employees first and stockholders second. Our firm could not change gears that fast, and besides, I disagreed with his priorities.

But it was not my company. I was a lowly outside consultant and admirer of Robert E. Thomas, founder and first chairman.

James C. Donnell, third-generation chairman of Marathon Oil, kept a diary of major and longtime stockholders, and he would call or go see them on his travels.

My first recommendation to him when I joined Marathon as a public relations manager was to put out year-end company operations feature news releases to newspapers, three months before the annual report. Jim was delighted at the knowledge and enthusiasm stockholders had from reading their year-end newspapers as he met them on his travels.

That stockholders are hungry for news of their investments is such an obvious truth, it should not have to be discussed. But few CEOs seem to know that and need to be reminded.

Stockholders like souvenirs from the operation, or even copies of significant news releases, new executive biographies with photos.

You must remember that the news media have no responsibility for publishing or broadcasting your news releases to your stockholders and other investors. Maybe you should buy ads, just to be sure—and conform to SEC prompt disclosure rules.

You need to remember that your largest potential market for your stock is the group of stockholders you already have.

An American Stock Exchange company got itself out of debt by offering stockholders a discounted third share for every two shares they already had.

Sometimes the stockholders could buy the stock from their broker cheaper than the checks they sent in to the company.

"Let's do it again!" said the chairman. ("Not on my watch," said the legal counselor.)

There is no end to creative thinking on stockholder information projects. Even plant tours or invitations to company executive speeches will be appreciated by your stockholders.

It pays even for a small company to have an employee specializing in stockholder communications, preferably somebody close to the management throne.

I end this brief discussion to remind you that you should <u>enjoy</u> communicating with your stockholders. They are nice folks as long as you do not kid them along, or promise them too much and give them too little. The investors you can worry about, as your company grows, are those institutional types who can become disenchanted and break your company in an afternoon. You might never learn the reason. Big executives of big companies praise institutional investors, even like those financial analysts who compliment in one breath, and curse in the next.

Be wise, kind and creative. Like hemorrhoidal bankers, those with money to invest cannot be taken for granted.

And don't be naive in dealing with analysts. After all, they are seeking your secrets to be put to use for sales profits to themselves.

They can help or hurt you, depending entirely on how you handle yourself with them.

We used to work for a NYSE-listed company with an executive vice president who lost his lunch every time he had to talk by phone with an analyst or *Wall Street Journal* reporter.

9

CROOKS USE PUBLIC RELATIONS

Just recently I broke off a conversation with a prospective client who called for an appointment, saying he had a gold mining patent earning him $12,000 a day. He added he could well pay for public relations help to become better known.

He suggested a rural truck stop cafe requiring an hour's drive for us both from different directions.

He explained his process for obtaining gold dust from gold-bearing desert rocks and sand.

He said he had a public stock offering prepared that the broker never got out, and I began to see why.

Then he offered to sell 20 per cent of his company for $250,000, if I knew of anybody.

My suggestion: "Prove your patented process works and get some mining trade publicity; then the investors will come to you. Don't humble yourself by beating the bushes for investors when you don't yet have the needed credibility."

Several years ago, a stock broker brought us a client who lied about everything from the very start, including a tour through his downtown Dallas office building under construction. None of his references checked out; in fact, they did him harm.

In five months, we were paid twice, and both times in Krugerands only coin shops would bid on.

In fact, the Dallas building was somebody else's, and our client did not even own the patent to make the machines that investors were putting money up for stock to manufacture. It was an absolute fraud!

I called the lead brokerage firm making a market for the company's stock, and the chairman screamed over my "negative attitude because we have hundreds of thousands of our own and clients' money in that company."

Now the brokerage firm and the phony company are both down the tube.

My instinct at the outset was that we were dealing with criminal bums all round.

One of my associates served on a rehabilitation board for recently released state prison inmates. One of his students came to our office in a rush, waited for an hour, then took a brochure and ran away. He said he had a confidential problem to discuss, but not with me.

Oh, well...

I heard his name later that afternoon on the radio. He had been arrested on a kidnapping charge related to abducting a business executive for ransom in another city.

The head of a Dallas cable television network came to see me on a client's recommendation. After a brief visit, he asked for my business card to take with him. "Are you considering hiring us?" I asked.

"No," he said, "I will need it when and if I get arrested around here. You just never know."

We never heard from him again.

We became associated with a U. S. Marshal who beat up a farmer in my presence over a quail hunting disagreement. He finally sued the farmer for stealing his shotgun during the confusion. When I heard about the suit, I called the Marshal and asked if I could help with the case since I was present. "Hell, no!" he replied. "You would just tell the truth."

Perhaps this discussion does not belong in the "crooks" chapter, but so often we run into insincere, irreverent connections with God or Jesus in client discussions.

This is because, as I keep saying, we are dealing with intangibles. Religion is an intangible also.

I worked one time for a clinical psychologist turned association executive. He told anyone who disagreed with him, "You don't believe in God, so how can I even discuss it with you?"

Another time at another place, the managing director of a company seeking to employ us for work in England suddenly said, "You have not yet met our Chairman of the Board." He passed to me a dinner plate with a color likeness of Jesus on it.

From then on he sought to get help without paying for it, but he said he mentioned us often in his "talks with the Chairman."

We have been associated with several evangelists who spoke to us often of God, and we had to take extreme measures short of lawyers with one to collect $140,000 owed for six months work devoted to a faith-healing hospital dedication publicity program.

The governor of a Midwestern state led in kneeling around his desk, asking God for help. (The governor went to prison a couple years later, perhaps still praying for help that never came.)

A very sincere business executive and a physician set up a manufacturing company after God sent the message on how to do it in a daily prayer. We had to hold back our enthusiasm, mixing religion, business and medicine in the public eye. One slip and the whole project could be looked at as preposterous, bearing no credibility. And medicine involves public health. It's risky stuff, indeed.

Regardless of how sharp a manager of people you are, and how well you think you know human nature, somebody wearing a scarlet letter will get by you occasionally—as well as to you.

A Christian gentleman got to be chairman of the board of a really big conglomerate company with many diverse operating subsidiaries. The top guy did not know a lot of businesses, but he did know people.

A subsidiary president called me to his office once, shut the door and unloaded that he wanted at once a good lawyer who did not know his chairman. I thought of one, a guy who hardly knew anybody. He was a real recluse but with great academic and moral credentials.

It seems the executive was toying with a secretary in his plant, and she decided it was worth $40,000, which she wanted in cash or she would blab.

The blackmailed executive called the lawyer who said, mainly, don't pay her anything since blackmail is a criminal offense.

A week later, the subsidiary president told me that he no longer needed the lawyer; he had fixed the problem himself.

"I just told her last night that I knew where her mother and her son live and I would have them both knocked off if she didn't let me alone. Except for nocturnal orgies, that is."

The lawyer didn't believe it, but a few months later, the chairman casually mentioned that he had had to terminate the subsidiary president because of immoral conduct reported from an investor in another city who knew of an event there involving a prostitute.

"Yeah," I said and told him of the president's problem with the secretary and its resolution.

The chairman, rightly, I think now, took issue with me over the handling of the blackmail affair. "If you had told me, even in confidence, we might have helped this poor man who now is unemployed."

Then he said I was the twenty-fourth associate who had told him—now—of the president's antics, all sexual.

I owed the top guy the information, though given to me confidentially and with professional trust, but I doubt if we could have helped the sex-driven official much. He lived and eventually died for pleasure.

10

AND GOVERNMENT LEADERS USE IT, TOO

The only reason I have added this short chapter is because you might wonder why I didn't. Government relations become a part of every CEO's working life, even his social life.

I have had more than my share of dealing with public office-seekers, all hoping or planning not to pay me unless they won.

I have had creative lies from office-seekers, really more than the incumbents, for obvious reasons. I have been between federal laws and government officials as the latter did not do their reporting jobs and ran out on me when the press came calling. I have seen CEOs obsessed with digging up money to give politicians, naively believing it was a good and safe, even patriotic, investment. Several are in jail because they believed erroneously and were abandoned by the political figures. Office-seekers can be cold, cold personalities when they want to be. They will gladly destroy you for your devoted support before they will admit to being in the wrong.

It is really hard to believe.

We had a political figure retain us on others' money and then asked me to go to the media with the story that his home, office and auto had been bugged by a known opponent for public office. I refused on the grounds that it was a police matter. He had wanted me to pass on a lie, unable to prove what he claimed. Of course, it was a cheaply concocted hoax for political gain.

I recently went to a U. S. senator to remind him that he had never announced in his hometown 40 new jobs from a Federal government agency opening an office there. "Of course not," he proclaimed. "I had to close the office from 40 miles away, and I don't want those folks thinking I am capitalizing on their bad luck at losing the office and jobs."

The Federal agency director said, "That other city paid no attention to us, and in our new location we are more important because we are closer to our market to serve. I will announce it myself."

Who really understands how myopic, single-minded and selfish political figures can be!

And even when they find a way to repay you for your work and investment in their popularity at the polls, they may be breaking the law, and you will become the goat in a striped suit on a rock pile.

It is awful to contemplate that our free-society republic is based on such truly dishonest shenanigans by unproductive human beings, who are able best to hoodwink us.

The one freedom I do not like is the freedom for some politician to sucker me and my resources when he is actually supposed to be serving me.

11

SO YOU ARE INTERNATIONAL?

It is common knowledge that most companies should be international in one way or another, whether they're in manufacturing or marketing, or finance.

It is a struggle for Americans to accept the business cultures outside the U. S. American oilmen learned a lot when in the 1980s they raced overseas "with empty suitcases" to get old family money from eager investors interested highly speculative oil deals, risky at best but better understood by American investors.

Millions of dollars were squandered on American oil operators by investors hopeful and a little greedy, much from Switzerland, the United Kingdom and Kuwait.

One of the London banking lordships put family money into an American oil company whose management had no idea who he was. He was brought to Tulsa and kept in a hotel room four days while company management told him very little about how they were spending his money. He went home and said "I sorta like those chaps but do not like the way they use my money."

The CEO of the oil company said flippantly: "Well, you can't please everybody. What the hell is a lord anyway, something out of the Bible?"

So much for Okie mentality.

No matter what you do overseas, you first need a national to be your legal counselor. Public relations is important, but overseas it is so unrefined by U. S. standards that you wind up with a lot of human and professional conflicts that make work impossible.

Our company long ago established a subsidiary in England, and for five years we tried to work with the wrong type of "solicitor". We were too busy promoting to notice until the head of Lazard Brothers told me we were in the wrong law pew. Our solicitor specialized in family relations and not corporate, and certainly not public relations.

We found a law firm specializing in American companies with British interests but who have little personal presence there. The solicitors do it all.

I called a meeting of some of our public relations associates, all British, at the solicitor's office and went merrily down a road of dreams about growing together on our U. S. money and expertise.

Finally, the lead solicitor shut down the meeting and took me out of the room for a hallway visit.

"You are far too generous with these chaps," he advised. "As soon as you go back to America, these fellows will try to take the company away from you. They are more desperate than you believe to get their hands on your assets."

I backed off, and he turned out to be right. The managing director we appointed and gave stock and money to got himself elected to a non-profit professional office and spent a year working the country for prestige and on our time and money. We went broke there even with U. S. clients going over for paying work and our U.K. staff was too busy even to see them. By the time we bounced the managing director and his staff, he had run up debt we would not pay from the U. S. It took accountants and solicitors to straighten it out but we learned our lesson well. In Switzerland and Spain, it went entirely different because we were dealing with less grabby public relations people, although the ways of doing things were entirely different—and not just language.

A Spanish petroleum refinery was boycotted by its workers, mostly peasant-level employees with new technical training, because the frame houses of the townspeople were always burning down and the refinery could not, by law, send out its firetruck. All turned out happily when the public relations people suggested the refiner buy another fire truck just for the town. Happiness reigned, the refinery manager was honored, and employee prospects lined up at the gate.

Across the Mediterranean in Libya, there was another problem brewing for public relations. The Libyans did not trust foreigners at work in the oilfields, and the foreigners found the Libyan "ragheads" distasteful because most of them could not read or write…or snort scotch.

But they all listened to the radio, and it was proposed that "wonderful world of oil" messages be played on commercial time on the radio stations. Know what oil management did? They authorized English language ads of compliments to be run in Libyan English language newspapers. The publishers soon caught on and began to charge for English language news releases they received and <u>sometimes</u> published.

The same oil companies marketers committed the same sort of error with people in Italy, like building service stations were most of the traffic was donkeys, some with carts and some without.

Never send an American to a foreign country to implement a public relations program without trustworthy and properly U. S.-oriented training.

We brought a Swiss national to the U. S. and found he could speak English much better than he understood it. He had even worse problems in Switzerland working with American clients, casually setting up news conferences with the wrong people attending. Koreans of Geneva were brought in from a cocktail lounge just to swell the crowd hearing a U. S. company chairman talk in Zurich.

Even in England, we had a client chairman from the U. S. speak at a black-tie dinner at a fashionable St. James Street 18th-century club. We staffed it with two Englishmen on our payroll, and the one thing they neglected to do was invite the press. Our client enjoyed himself but the press was angered we did not let them know.

"Thank the Lord, we were on the job for the dinner," our U. K. staffer said on the phone the next day. "The club employees had the chairs set up all wrong, some behind posts, so my associate and I put a stop to that and moved them rightly around."

It reminded me of a news conference and luncheon we had for Texas clients at the New York "21" Club. The waiters kept the meeting going from 12 to 5 with numerous gifts and special desserts that both baffled and broke our clients who did go home and brag about the Texas-sized luncheon they had all afternoon at "21".

South American country media will cooperate if you pay them. In Mexico, public relations even in Mexico City is not well considered, except by the few English language newspapers. The mañana attitude exists even in business and the media, with long lunch hours and lots of cocktails. The Mexican public relations types, like so many without U. S. business sophistication, literally steal your resources under false pretense.

It's the same old philosophy around the world that we have brought on ourselves with our political philosophy of trying to support the whole world with U. S. taxpayer money.

In public relations, with all the intangibles, it is easier to get the money from Americans based on windy promises. Once I had an alleged banker from Belgium come see me about meeting my clients so he could refinance them with European money looking for American company homes. We thought he was funny, the way he carried on, but introduced him to a needy client chairman who thought he was funny also. It seems the Belgian was promising money to be delivered <u>after</u> he got hold of company assets.

The FBI came calling on me three months after the investor graced my office and said he was a swindler on a world scale. I erred by observing, "He seemed like such a nice fellow!"

The agent remarked, "That's the problem, sir."

It takes a lot of patience and realistic goals for overseas public relations to succeed, and one major problem is that we Americans just plain have too much money and waste it. For every dollar we spend on foreign public relations help that does not perform the way we hoped, three more dollars are being sought by desperate, hungry practitioners whose only objective is to get your faith, confidence and money.

Only the English will take your money and sass you about how uncouth you are socially. I had a long-time journalist friend who was a writer and BBC commentator who took my money and sought even more for things that never worked out to our satisfaction. One time he put on a news conference and buffet for an American client visiting London, and there were more waiters than guests. The Japanese were putting on a spiffier reception down the street, and their English PR people had done a better job of getting out a crowd. While I double-talked with the embarrassed client, my BBC friend hired a limo to go to Greenwich "on the town pub-hopping to get the client's mind off the buffet disaster."

Some years later, the BBC commentator got tired of my hanging around him with money, so he took me to a luncheon at his club and so paid me off for once and for all, and we parted company.

In conclusion, I am reminded of a British client we had stationed in the U. S. Service clubs liked the way he talked, so he received one special invitation from a large city's Economics Club. After his talk, he got a question: "How do you feel about the American economy?"

The Brit drew himself up proudly and retorted, "I try not to think about it since once we owned it all!"

If your company is so international, it probably hires nationals from the countries where you work to work in the U. S. Be warned that you can bring on unanticipated cultural-business problems.

A U. S. equipment broker for overseas markets hired a Tunisian with a U. S. college degree to sell in the Mid-East from the U. S. The first sale he made was in Kuwait, and he diverted the profit from the sale to a nephew attending college in Ohio. The way he looked at it, it was not stealing if it went to somebody more needy than the company.

Then we met an out-of-work Ph.D. who had headed an international service company until he decided, children grown, he would dwell on advanced education and work as little as possible. Our client hired him, and let him turn overseas sales trips into happy adventures for the employee and his wife.

Management learned better, partly by having a public relations analysis done on new employee prospects. "Are these employees about to stand up under public scrutiny?"

12
HOW MUCH DOES IT COST?

Public relations is a professional management service. It is easy to pay too much or too little.

Being an intangible, hot air and mystique can play a role in getting you to pay for what you may not get.

So often I have heard New York City PR consultants impress, say, Kansas publicly held company executives with such talk as, "We talk to Wall Street every day about stock in your company and the price should soon hit the ceiling."

Hogwash.

An Ohio CEO was promised a *Time* magazine cover, and the consultants even had dummied up a cover with his photo on it. They did not remain friends and business associates for long.

When you hire staff, it is like buying the services of accountants or lawyers, depending on experience and good things said by previous employer references. Some of those you hire are outstanding. Some are routine. It is presumed anybody you would hire is competent, at least. But let's consider character and integrity.

Over one hundred thousand dollars a year is reasonable for retainer or hourly charge totals for international counsel and basic program implementation.

When you shop around for consultants or employees, do not seek "price". You usually do get what you pay for, if you know what you are seeking and with whom you are dealing.

Remember, the spokespeople you hire must be responsible communicators because they can do you more damage than good once they are officially on board and accepted by opinion leaders.

As public relations prestige increases in business, so does the value of the practitioners. A shabby public relations employee reflects poorly on your company and its management.

An experienced employee is worth about $50,000 a year and a director or manager over $100,000.

Consultant fees should run over $100 per hour, even $200 per hour or more for exceptional experience. Their value is in the millions of dollars, if you use them right, treat them right.

Remember, your public relations people, inside and out, carry your secrets, and you do not want them unhappy with your show of loyalty and appreciation through compensation, among other things.

Losing an effective PR associate is a big loss—one difficult to remedy.

And their bad-mouthing you is what you don't need.

Take care...

13

WHERE DOES ADVERTISING COME IN?

Advertising people are different from public relations people, often like night and day, Mutt and Jeff.

Ad people are marketing-oriented; PR people are image-oriented and perhaps publicity-biased.

Ad space and air time, even direct mail, are vehicles of communication, like books and pamphlets…even sky-writing. The message is controlled by the buyer, effective with the audiences depending on the message and the message sender.

PR people fly by the seat of their pants, while ad people are serious planners, often clever.

PR people worry about credibility since what they are selling is more intangible and may be shunted aside for trivial reasons or whims or emotions.

Corporate advertising, especially the kind called "institutional," is a good tool, like Mobil Oil telling the petroleum story so well for so long with well-written editorial columns.

Marketing advertisers are not good at the corporate story even in ads, but journalists in PR do it right.

I saw the giant ad agency N. W. Ayer strike out on a corporate ad account because it tried to sell the corporate story like selling toothpaste. Hill & Knowlton stepped in, protesting they were not ad people, and they did it well. (But they had to refund the ad commissions to the client since they were already collecting a hefty retainer plus hourly time charges.)

Let me say this right now. Top management is in charge of the overall image of the company of which advertising, even product, is part of the set of tools. Policy is set at the top, so top management should never let go of any of the tools since it is easy for one company to be telling the public two different stories.

It is silly for more than one overall ad policy. Just one is enough, covering the institutional as well as product messages.

CEO's like this policy if they can understand its importance and get hold of it and keep it while doing it right.

One chief executive I know liked public relations so well, and was so good at it, he wiped out his company's advertising department and created seven different clients, mostly products and services, for the savvy PR firm to handle. The CEO, of course, was the company's public relations director in function.

What ticked him off to drastically change communicators was when he found the ad department spending over $50,000 on a campaign to sell in a market it already had 80 per cent of.

14

STRANGE PUBLIC RELATIONS ACTIVITIES BY MANAGEMENT

The larger the company, the bigger the public relations goofs of management.

It is almost as if managements often think the public and the media are blind, along with law-enforcement agencies protecting investors, like the SEC.

Lots of managements do not <u>fear</u> their companies being ignored by the public; they just want to be left alone.

An electric company spent $2 million on a goose-hunting preserve just for members and staff of the state utilities commission. A retired sheriff was manager and caretaker. They imported lumber to build the "longest bar in the world" in a club house where guests ate and drank between shooting geese that would land in a field to eat troughs of grain.

Two major oil companies found themselves in Alaska with a lot of natural gas and oil to sell. They created two corporate entities, one a pipeline for transporting gas and the other a natural gas utility company. Without consulting anybody with public relations responsibilities, the managements appointed local business and government leaders to directorships in the two companies.

Then came the marketing woes, chiefly U. S. military bases that kept burning coal. Gas was much cleaner and cheaper to burn. Even to get the coal to market, mine owners had to depend on a Department of the Interior train.

The military base commanders were in no hurry to change since Alaskan coal operators had a lot of power. The natural gas folks were newcomers, not yet politically established.

The general counsel of one of the majors dispatched a public relations manager who formerly was an investigative reporter for a metropolitan newspaper to find out what was wrong. Even the two Alaskan company boards seemed powerless.

Amazing. The men appointed to the directorships had big coal interests and strong connections with Washington, D. C. No wonder gas was not moving, and no wonder the military bases had long-term coal contracts.

When the oil company lobbyists began work on the waste of taxpayers' money, scandal was narrowly averted.

Before the matter was resolved and natural gas was flowing to the military bases, bankers had become involved. Nothing moves without bankers' money and bankers, even if there is fraud, waste and public deception involved.

When threatened with exposure, the two company boards of directors ranted and fought but had to go along, mainly perhaps because the oil companies began to pay them better for losing interest in coal.

A major auto manufacturer agreed to fly some public opinion and marketing executives from Detroit to Milwaukee for a national business convention program. The audience waited over an hour for the group to arrive, and the weather was turning sour. The corporate plane with the auto people was contacted by radio, circling Milwaukee.

"The folks for the program are all drunk, this bad weather and all," the pilot said. "Us crew members are beginning to drink, too, so I think we will just turn around and go back to Detroit."

Which they did. Next program, please.

The chairman of a NYSE-listed minerals company loaded a 20-pound smoked sturgeon on a plane, under his seat in a wrapper, and took off for New Jersey to call on an investor. The investor took the sturgeon and bought some stock, but the next month he sued the company for fraud. The chairman had since retired, however, so *Fortune* magazine got to run the photo of the new chairman being welcomed aboard with a civil law suit caused by his predecessor. Unfortunately, the suit was thrown out of court after repeated diminishing offers of settlement from the plaintiff. The new chairman, by now experienced in the case, declined his public relations consultant's recommendation of issuing a news release saying that the suit had been thrown out. "I am so sick of it all that I don't even want to announce the good news from it," he said.

The chairman of a large manufacturing company established some working relationships with a similar firm in Germany, so it invited him and his wife over to Europe for some business ceremonies. The American couple showed up in the wrong apparel, and the man was puffing at his pipe, which had the bowl turned down and sparks and ashes were floating all over. The couple tottered and reeked of martinis. They were hustled back to their limo and back to their hotel, and the whole business venture fell apart. The Germans know how to get things done even if it is social, but the loose-jointed Americans make it easy because there is so little respect for the rigidity of foreign cultures.

A Swiss investor with gangland connections in South America married a Brazilian prostitute and moved her to Geneva. He put on a gala ball honoring her, and nobody came but the Americans who thought it was a cool thing for the old man to do. The host grumbled, "but the guests I really didn't care about coming were the Americans, who talk and drink too much."

So much for the recycled whore incident. She had feelings, too, and they were hurt—mainly by the Americans who showed up out of curiosity.

In South Bend, Indiana, a federal court there held an antitrust trial of a dozen companies for alleged price-fixing. The judge impaneled the jury and told them, "Keep lots of pens and paper with you since it will be a long trial and you need to take lots of notes."

A young executive raced from the audience to the jury box with sacks of paper pads and pens, all advertising materials from a major company, handing it out by the handfuls to the smiling jurors.

The judge sent all the public relations people for the defendant companies home, souvenirs and all.

15

PLEASE DON'T KILL THE MESSENGER

When you get involved in a public relations activity, you automatically set up an intelligence network, bringing back information to you as well as disseminating it.

Be mature enough to appreciate it. Use it. Don't reject it, and don't abuse it.

You can learn a lot by listening.

It is a way of knowing your audience before you speak to it.

Professional communicators, as public relations people are, can tell you a lot you should know.

Some CEOs may reject this as gossip. Others just don't want to hear any news unless it is positive, perhaps even flattering.

(Now is the time to re-read the fable, "The Emperor's New Clothes.")

We had a fourth-generation CEO of a large supply company who hated gossip even when it was true and in his best interests to listen. He was a corporate spoiled brat who finally gave up the strain of business and sold out. Another CEO was a physician who had gone into homeopathic drug manufacturing and marketing. He could not be told anything; he knew it all. Financially, he was stretched thin, and his payables were going so long that his creditors began to talk about him behind his back. Should they be cautious, worry a little, ask for payment in advance? The public relations consultant gave him a written report on all this, and it angered him. He said the consultant was disloyal. So the relationship was terminated, leaving the doctor to mutter about the problems he had were really the faults of others—like lazy warehousemen who would not keep store shelves filled with his medicines.

The medicines were overpriced for what they did over a long period of time. Competition offered results faster, cheaper.

So he cut the overhead to raise the profit, and first to go was the advertising.

You can imagine the business disaster.

What did the doctor do? He invested himself into the power of prayer. He also sold stock to patients, employees and friends.

The negative word-of-mouth talk about the doctor's products soon caught up with him, although he had been told in writing what was being said in the field. He simply killed the messenger.

Trust your PR people to keep you informed, sifting the facts from fiction (gossip), or enjoying both.

Several times in my early career days, I had older people use me as their source of inside information. I was immature enough to give it to them. Once one of my contacts gave me information I believed, and I nearly got fired over it. It was such hot information on labor relations inside the company that it was demanded of me to disclose my source. I was a clam-mouth. The company management made a U-turn in labor relations and called off a pay raise for management. This was misuse of a little intelligence network. I was an instrument of damage within a fine company with serious labor problems, very adversarial.

Be careful how you pull young PR people in over their heads. But maturely use your own intelligence network.

And now is a good time to mention again, without seeking your admonishing for possible breach of ethics (like blackmail), that once you hire PR experts, in-house or outside counsel, you can expect their loyalty only so long as you are loyal to them. My life of experiences in the field is riddled with clients or bosses who suddenly felt they could dish out abuse to the opinion-makers and still expect their dedication and loyalty.

Where have you been for the last one hundred years?

Loyalty, like public relations itself, is a two-way street.

I think it is possible that even rattlesnakes get to feeling "enough is enough" and smile before striking a victim, perhaps once a friend—or client or boss.

Why should professional king-makers (communicators) be loyal to you when you are not loyal to them? (Most client shaftings are over $$.) Too few client-types seem to understand this. Hire some communicators, treat them fine, throw them out—and expect to hear them continuing to say nice things about the now disloyal clients.

No, where have you been the last <u>two</u> hundred years?

16

JUDGMENT

Nothing puts your executive judgment to the test like managing that intangible called public relations.

Should you announce what you think is important (news) or wait for some news medium to call?

If you decide to announce it, should you let radio, TV, the trade press, magazines or newspapers have the break on it?

Or just call a news conference, inviting them all?

Is it big enough news for a news conference?

First, let me say the one thing worse than not calling a news conference with good reason is to call one and have nobody show up.

What you need to answer this question is knowledge of what news is, how the importance of your "news event" meshes with the other happenings, and how you will present what you have to say.

The CEO of a new and successful Houston company (with lots to brag about to the media) hosted a news conference with luncheon at the Houston Club. Everybody howdied, sat down and ate lunch: fine steaks with fresh strawberries flown in from France that morning. I was a guest and sat with the press, all of us shifting nervously for the announcements to begin. But the luncheon concluded with just a thank-you for coming from the CEO and no passing out of announcement papers.

It was a washout, but the CEO beamed.

"Somebody ought to fax those news people something," I said to the CEO. "Oh, we will, we will," he said. "Weren't those strawberries delicious?"

This incident of frustrating the news media had nothing to do with it, but the CEO was replaced a few months later.

It was worse for me because the company retained public relations counsel I knew, but the counsel was not trade-news oriented.

The CEO didn't know big city news people eat the luncheons with sources of news. Because the host company was well known as a fast-starter in industry service and technology, the media turned out in great numbers.

News conferences take a lot of planning, with the emphasis on "news."

This was a costly and absolutely counterproductive effort that made the company look bad, not good.

It was bad judgment even to hold a news conference.

Use of judgment in public relations administration and planning is like walking a tightrope, balancing yourself this way and that to get to your destination.

A wrong phone call can put the CEO into jail and/or ruin the company's credibility.

As you run a company, your decisions involve the money of others—investors, customers, etc. It becomes fraud when you slip or cheat, or appear to do so. Money management involves taxes, and that involves, you guessed it, the IRS.

Today, the pressure on CEO judgments are more intense than ever. A lighthearted comment can lead to racial discrimination or sexual harassment charges.

I recently heard a psychiatrist give a talk in which he said that the only really safe way to answer a question anymore is with another question.

I witnessed a chairman address his company officers, and he was so disorganized that his vice presidents took to correcting him from the audience.

And one time our firm was hired by a company president to write him a speech for a company management weekend retreat "so powerful they will have to respect me for the job I am trying to do as their leader."

I suggested that instead of such a speech, he might be better off by spilling his guts to the chairman of the family-dominated company. "Just ask him to get the others off your back!" I suggested.

We wrote the speech, three times, and he gave it, got his applause and compliments…then resigned.

Through the years, I have noticed that it takes some aging on the job for the CEO to hone his judgment. One CEO I worked for was so full of booze after lunch that he could be right about everything but never get credit for it.

We had a former newsman, an award-winner, working for us in Seattle who was truly right in all he did and said, but he drank a lot and you could smell it…as he poked his finger into your chest to emphasize how right he was. Yes, it was bad judgment for him to drink, and it eventually destroyed him.

Nothing is more important to image-building than judgment: even how you dress, get your hair styled, and the kind of language you use.

One time we had a client CEO who loved to shock his directors by shouting at his secretary, "Hazel, damnit, get your hands out of my drawers!"

The Dallas directors laughed, but the ones from Boston didn't.

Occasionally, a CEO has told the press too much, perhaps in confidence, not knowing they do not have to accept his "off the record, of course."

A company I knew was spending hundreds of thousands of dollars to find a new corporate identity—name and logo and business service policy with new goals.

The principal trade magazine in the industry sought the new name in advance, even in confidence.

The CEO gave it to the editor—in confidence.

The magazine ran the story, cautiously worded, and company executives ran around several days pointing fingers at one another over who blabbed.

The CEO called a meeting and admitted it was he and was glad he did. "Keeping secrets from our friends is silly," he said.

But God help any other executive who would have done it. The CEO had good public relations sense and kept his PR people and outside counsel under-informed. Some chief executives are like that. I would defend their right to be what they are since they do not louse up the corporate profile by keeping silly secrets that are in the best company interests to be publicly known.

Just worry about your judgment being right most of the time, or use your judgment to get good advice based on others' better judgment.

I don't like bill collectors and their sneaky ways, but we needed one once. A company hired us to do art work for a sales brochure and never paid for it. Worse, they framed the art for the lobby of its offices because it was so proud of it. As our chase heated up, the company abruptly moved their offices to Dallas.

I found a collection agency from the Dallas Yellow Pages and called it. The man answering the phone said, yes, he could make one call for us at the company and would guarantee payment in full for a modest fee. He did, and I was impressed, so I asked him how he did it, as I mailed him his check.

"We have never met, have we?" he asked. "Well, I am nearly eight feet tall, red-haired and pock-marked, and I must weigh 330 pounds. Get it?"

Yeah. One of the company principals called me up with curses for our techniques.

Ironic, isn't it?

17

DEATH CAN BE A PROBLEM

A client came to us for help promoting his company's 50th anniversary and his personal 35th anniversary with the company.

We started the budget with $300,000 and as his enthusiasm grew with the planning of market surveys, new logo, and institutional advertising, he would ante up more at $100,000 a throw.

It was an international service company, so we did an international survey of their customers and got their input on how the company had changed in half a century.

The results were amazing. The customers ranked an obscure company service highest, something management had overlooked. It was too obvious.

Three approaches to a new logo were commissioned to three different art studios, one in London.

The ads were designed and radio-TV spots cut.

Suddenly the CEO died, and as consultants, we were doomed. The new CEO was from outside, and he turned our program over to an inexperienced PR director whom we had left out of our program development at the request of the late CEO.

The debate over contracts, budgets, bills and the future of the program grew pretty intense. Luckily, the general counsel of the company had been close to the late CEO, but as consultants, we were "outsiders" compared with the in-house PR manager.

The program went on without the professionalism that went into the different aspects of it…even billboards for the major office cities. It all became cheap-o to prove a good corporate program could be conducted without outside hotshots who "charged big fees for everything." It was a costly mess mainly, without the CEO sparkplug who had helped plan it and wanted to play a role in it. It was in his image.

The company went out of business and had only a couple of lawyers handling litigations, the last time I heard.

Obviously the moral of this episode is that every company client should have a #2 and #3 on such a program, not just a CEO and public relations counselor who got along so well.

18
ETHICS

When to tell the press everything and when to keep a secret.

I do not mean to be evasive but it all depends. You should anticipate the results of what you might do before you do anything.

Here is an example you can identify with.

The branch vice president of a company headquartered far away was under the gun with a jealous boss. The VP needed some clippings to make his achievements apparent. He had recently hit a company home run and his PR manager talked to the business editor about doing a Sunday feature on the remarkable achievement.

Two days before the trip with the editor, the VP got word his office would be closed in six months. Should the editor be told? He might cancel the interview, withdraw the offer of recognition the VP so hungered for.

The trip and interviews went so well, the editor began to wonder about the...closing the office.

The story was superb but the VP was about to be canned anyway, and when the closure was announced a few days after the Sunday feature, everybody involved looked bad. The editor will never fully trust anybody like that again. The VP still wonders if he did right or wrong. The PR manager, now, knows he erred by not taking the editor into his confidence, hoping, praying the story would go through anyway.

Yes, the editor should have been trusted.

19
BOOZE

It is hard to think of anything good to say about alcohol and public relations.

Public relations is a stressful business, one requiring clear minds without obstructions.

Unfortunately, imbibing in booze gives one the illusion of being strong and creative, scribbling great ideas and peoples' names on cocktail napkins—which cannot be read the next morning.

A big company's public relations manager called me with great enthusiasm one afternoon. His company had had to terminate their best staff man in public relations, after 17 years, because of a personality conflict with a higher executive who was wrong. They wanted me to hire the wonderful PR guy. We did after an interview.

It was obvious after a few weeks on the job that the guy had a drinking problem, in and out the back door to his car and nursing a coffee cup all day long.

Finally, with the chairman and president of our best client, he passed out reeking in a mayor's office.

The client executives were compassionate, recalling such instances in their business lives.

Another large company parted with their public relations vice president in a more unique way...they gave him a big country club, black-tie farewell party. He fell drunk on the way home after blacking one of his wife's eyes. The same man had disappeared at a company news conference and was found, head in toilet, in the women's rest room. Another time in another city, he spent the night at a sin-den of women of another color and culture.

Once soon after retirement he came to see us and an old friend visitor, and fell over a massive stone ash tray in our lobby.

We twisted and turned to find a productive relationship since his "friends in high places" would return the favor, but everything we considered was a joke. Besides, he did not wish to work at the business anymore, just have fun.

We had a large client with a Chairman who was red-faced from alcohol flush 20 hours of the day. But he was sharp of mind and fists. At an informal company dinner, he nagged at me over my pronouncing certain names and I thought he was kidding from down in his cups. A director finally whispered to me: "Better move away, he's preparing to hit you. He always ends discussions of disagreement with his fists." I often wonder…

When alcohol enters the room, good judgment leaves.

I worked for a large advertising agency as Public Relations Director. I was assigned to accompany a client Vice President, our boss, on a trip to a New Jersey city. The client had a snoot full (on my tab) when he insulted our waitress by telling her she was ugly and, besides, "you have a crooked nose."

We retired to our low-budget twin-bedded hotel room. In early hours of the morning, I was awakened by a noise like the grinding squeak of an unoiled door hinge. I blinked and in the moonlight on the other bed, I could see our client masturbating, fully exposed in the moonlight with his covers pushed back. He was gritting his teeth most vigorously.

Back home the next day, all was honey and roses, nothing seemingly remembered from the night before.

I had gotten some sleep by putting my head beneath the pillow.

A few years later, overseas with an American tycoon in love and business, I had to listen through the wall as he romanced an "Egyptian princess" he had picked up—or so was being said through the wall.

A management duo from Argentina, in the U.S. to address a management convention, asked me "where are the women?" immediately upon their plane landing. I struck out trying to explain I was no pimp.

A month after they went home, I received an autographed picture of himself from one of them: "To Dingo from his South American friend who lifts himself from his bed every morning with his front-side hydraulic lift."

20

A DOUBLE BEWARE

Remember that your public relations staffer or outside consultant cannot afford the American luxury of really disliking anybody like you can. (Or think you can.)

So you get yourself, or them, into politics where there is much emotional debate and somebody loses when somebody wins.

One cannot be in public relations and dislike anybody.

I have known many business careers destroyed by mixing business professionalism with politics.

Even lawyers, quick as they are, often give up law careers to be political candidates. (When they lose, they go back to being lawyers, selling what they have learned to their clients and chasing after those with clout.) The gift of gab is strong public medicine.

A public relations counselor had given up an eastern state senator position to become what he was. Unfortunately, he thought he knew who had voted for and against him. The former were friends, the latter enemies. When his friends in government would get him a state contract, his enemies eventually would take it away from him. His health failed and he got a nice appointment, but in a year the party in power changed and he lost it. Past sixty years old and back to the beginning—except for that growing number of people disliked.

Other businessmen in politics sold their friends out for votes on issues friends did not support. The business-political mix is poor.

To hell with friendship and business integrity, get that vote! Get that power!

If you are the boss calling the shots, your PR people must think as you do, dislike whom you dislike.

Lord help you when you come to dislike a broadcast news director or print editor.

Even if the news person has an elevator that does not go all the way up (as we say of those unbright folks) but he still is in power over you, your image, your reputation.

One metropolitan editor I knew for years kept a file in his desk on the intellectual, professional misdeeds of a high-up in public relations. He dreamed of going to the company president sometime and showing pounds of evidence on what a numbskull the PR guy was. He would even chortle in his sleep over that happy coming day of revenge.

But the PR fellow took early retirement and the editor gnashed his teeth in futility, but he likes to tell the story of the chase and the file he still has. He frets that the grim reaper will come calling on one of them before he settles the issue—pure intellectual revenge, retribution.

So in the interest of your good life and image, stay out of politics and don't get permanently mad at a news person.

Either can destroy you and all you stand for.

A fabulous governor of a state chose that political career and settled all problems with a few drinks. His calling could better have been evangelistic crusades. He died tragically. His name went from sunshine and valor to pure mud. He deserved better, nearly had it. What a waste!

EPILOGUE
NOW FOR SOME PUBLIC
RELATIONS HAPPY STORIES
(WELL, PARTLY HAPPY...)

Needing some patriotism in their image, petroleum industry leaders in Oklahoma built a $500,000 statue "Oil Patch Warrior" dedicated to World War II drillers in England. The British Minister of Energy participated in the dedication in 1991. President Bush, an oilman and World War II veteran, did not. Said an aide: "We fail to see the connection between oil and war."

◆　　◆　　◆　　◆　　◆

Ohio Oil Company at 75 years of age was tired of being confused with Standard Oil of Ohio, so it changed its name to a product brand name, Marathon. In six months, it was better known than ever, mainly because it ran institutional advertising telling the company history story.

Livingston Oil needed a name change, so it went with their NYSE stock symbol, LVO. Small ads, "LVO on the GROW" helped make the company popular with investors, and LVO eventually sold out with big profits to investors.

✦   ✦   ✦   ✦   ✦

An energy transmission company was organized after Canadians threatened to cut off its supplies to U. S. northern tier states. Hastily, a company supported by money from big corporations was organized, staffed primarily with retirees and rejects from the supporting companies. Internal politics took over, and the executives gave in to their ambitions. Pettiness reigned, and the company destroyed itself from the inside. Said the chairman: "Well, at least our competitors didn't get to do it."

✦   ✦   ✦   ✦   ✦

A geology consulting company was retained by big-money interests to study ways of pumping liquid wastes beneath the ground and into porous rock formations. The waste could be hidden forever or pumped out at a later time.

It was called Deep Well Disposal.

"Oh, we have a little pollution problem with our river," said one Chamber of Commerce official. "For sure, we have meat-packing plants working around the clock and pouring entrails and associated liquid wastes into a ditch six feet deep and six feet across, going directly into the river."

Another company making acid admitted putting old acids into its river, causing dead fish to cluster along miles of shoreline.

The geology company CEO went to Washington with the shocking pollution data, but nobody was interested.

Back to the plants surveyed. Nobody was interested in water pollution control.

Report to stockholders: "Nothing will be done until Congress makes the polluters behave better."

A hotel management company hired a PR firm to upgrade the image and business of a historic hotel. Building a publicity program around a chef-manager from Italy, the hotel built its Sunday brunch business up by 450 percent, while the room occupancy went up over 200 percent, despite lousy telephones, lumpy mattresses and maids with VD and habits of stealing from suitcases. Nevertheless, progress was made…until a sales agent booked a male homosexual beauty pageant. The PR firm found a way to cancel it. The CEO of the parent company, an engineer, grunted, "Absolutely not. We are in the business of renting rooms!"

For a week, local TV and newspapers had pictures of pickets waving signs, "Sodomy Is Sin."

The hotel went out of business, with no way of getting the public back.

A Denver cocktail lounge needed business, so it hired a PR firm at $1,000 a month, and it got lots of publicity bringing in hordes of new drinkers/munchers. But they did not drink much. Customers had just one or two drinks and ate lots of munchies. The PR firm even considered a topless dancer or nude waitresses but finally found a color stylist to examine the lounge's decor. Sure enough! The walls and ceiling were blue, a cool and refreshing color. It was repainted a torrid red, a hot and thirsty color. All became happy again as the crowds became thirstier and more friendly, with more waitresses serving more drinks to patrons almost panting for the cool and wet treat to their lips.

Stockholders in a small OTC company complained that they did not like the reading material put in the annual report. Instead of hiring better writers, the company increased the size of the typeface, and all was happy again. The corporate secretary had erred in making the type so small so stockholders would not go to the trouble to read it carefully. The bad idea backfired, didn't it?

This was the same corporate secretary who would not speak with financial reporters because "they are out to make me look bad." Actually, this philosophy made himself look bad. The reporters would just go to the CEO and call the secretary "a schnook" or worse.

The Chairman of a public company needed some foreign investors to balance out his American ones. After weeks of grooming for his investors' presentations, with charts, he rose up in Zurich and opened with…"I know none of you has ever heard of our company. Actually, we are just a fly-speck on the windshield of life…"

ABOUT THE AUTHOR

Dean Stratton Sims is a Kansan living in Oklahoma where he is Chairman and Chief Executive Officer of a public relations counseling firm he founded in 1965. Prior to that, he was a public relations manager for a major international oil company. He had been a public relations consultant in New York and Philadelphia after almost seven years as a public relations manager of a management association. He worked for various newspapers and the Associated Press until he heard that PR paid better and offered better working hours and benefits…like carpet and a secretary. He still freelances travel articles and book reviews, frequently making speeches on his experiences. He seeks to convince clients and prospects that he was put on earth to work hard to improve business communications for a happier, healthier private enterprise system, and a more satisfied public.

So long as he pays his annual dues, he is an accredited public relations practitioner (and counselor) by the Public Relations Society of
America.

0-595-25695-3

www.ingramcontent.com/pod-product-compliance
Lightning Source LLC
Chambersburg PA
CBHW021544200526
45163CB00015B/1513